Traveling Alaska

Artistic Images of Modes of Transportation in Alaska... To Color!

Brittney Kauffman

Copyright © 2018 by Brittney Kauffman

All rights reserved.
This book or any portion thereof may not be reproduced or used in any manner whatsoever without the express written permission of the artist.

First Printing, 2018

ISBN-10 1727380800

www.facebook.com/artbybrittneyk
inkedfoxak@gmail.com

Guidelines

1. Gently tear or cut the page of your choosing out of the coloring book.
2. Color your page using colored pencils, fine-tip markers, or fine-tip pens. It's your art, so these are just suggestions. (I personally use Staedtler marker pens)
3. Find the word 'Alaska' hidden in your drawing.
4. Display! Each page is 8x10 and one-sided for the purpose of being able to display your work, should you choose to do so. (8x10 is also a standard frame size)

Most of all, have fun!

Can't find 'Alaska' in your drawing? Look to the back of the book for help!

This coloring book is dedicated to my daughter, Charlotte, who loves airplanes and cars.

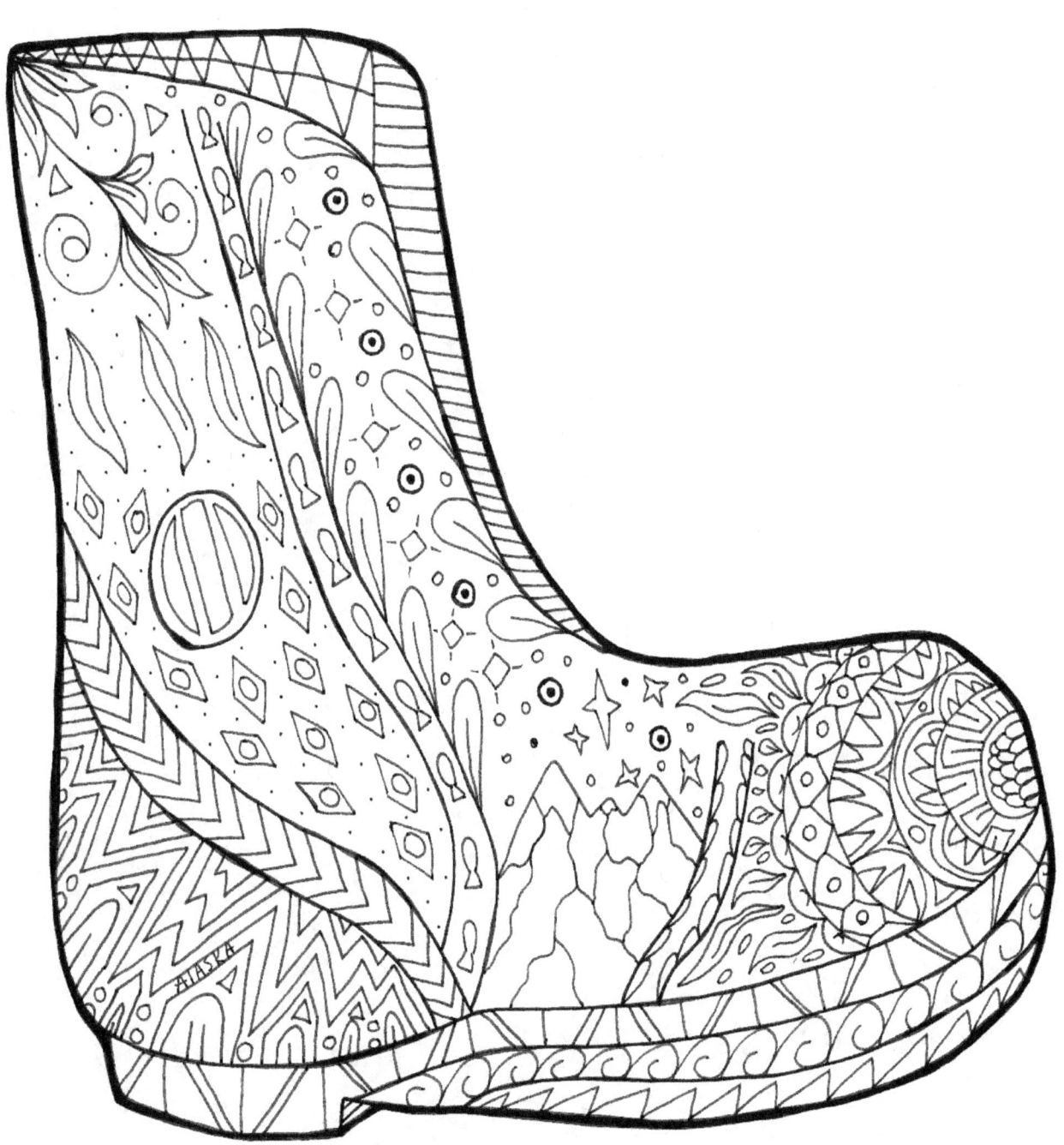

Winter Boot
"Bunny Boot"

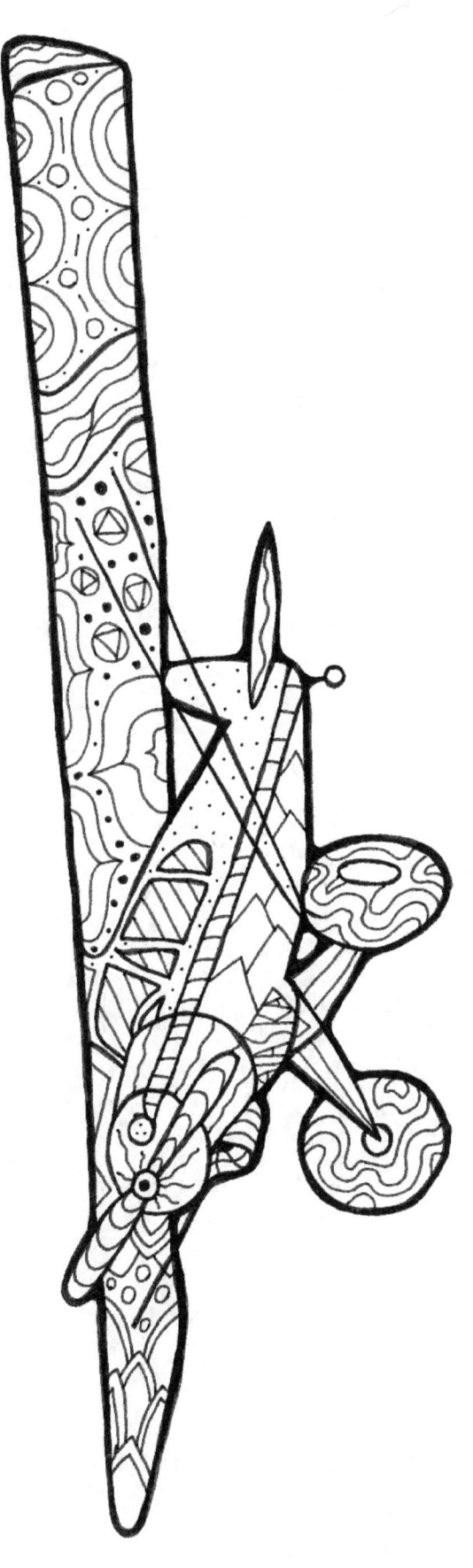

Bush Plane

There are many places in Alaska that can be accessed only by plane.

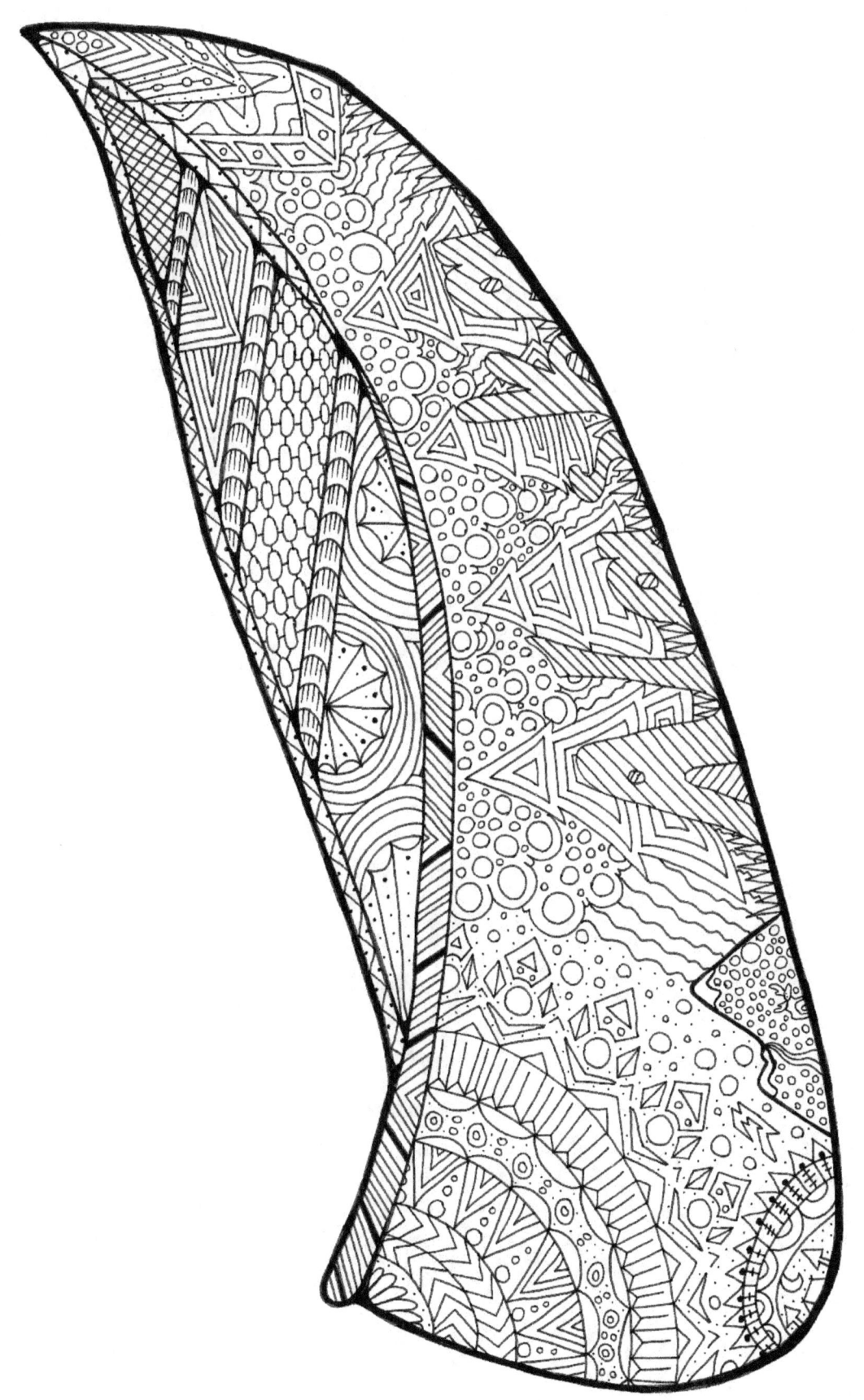

Canoe

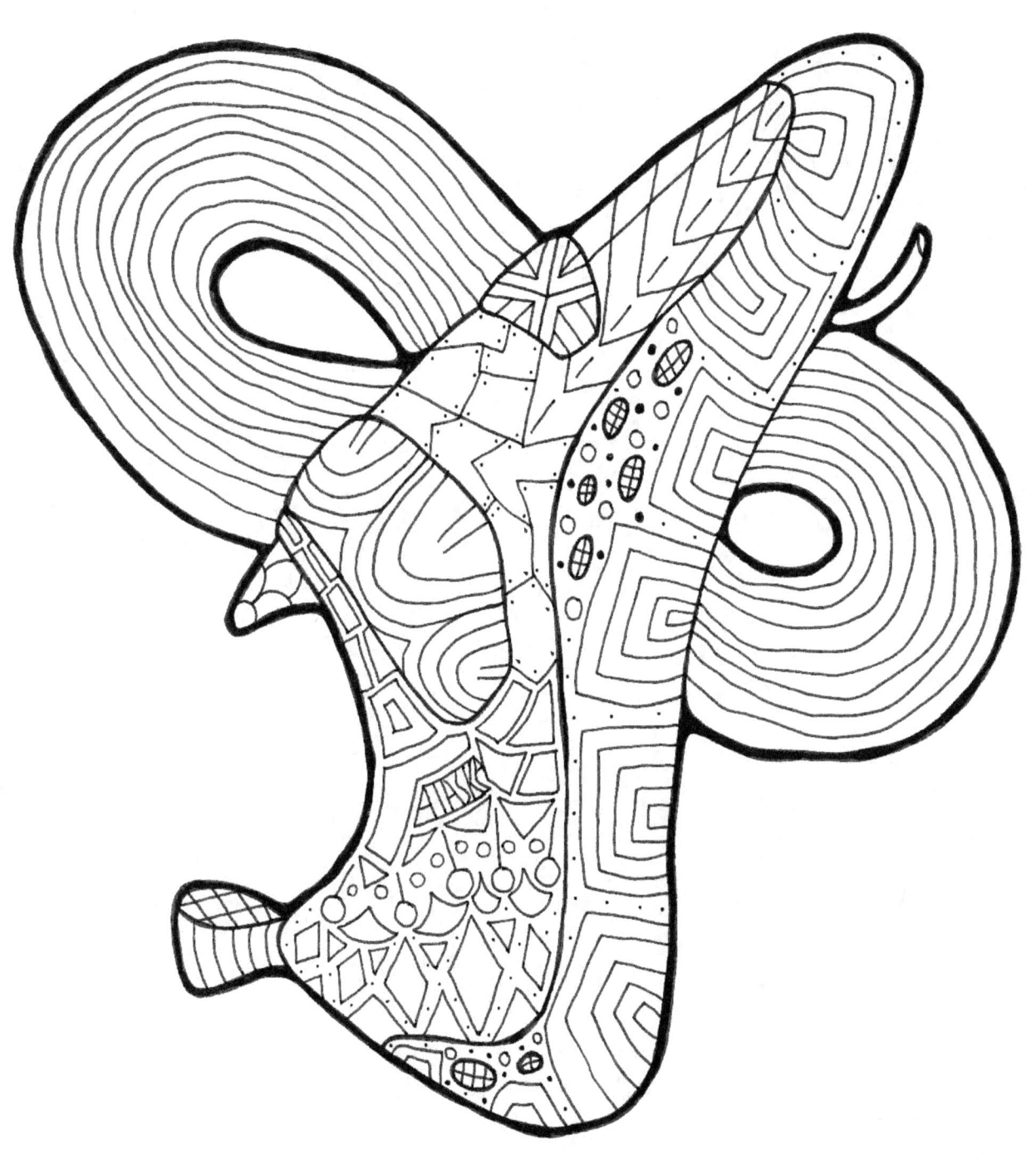

Climbing Shoe and Rope

Rock climbers can be spotted along the side of the road in some areas of Alaska

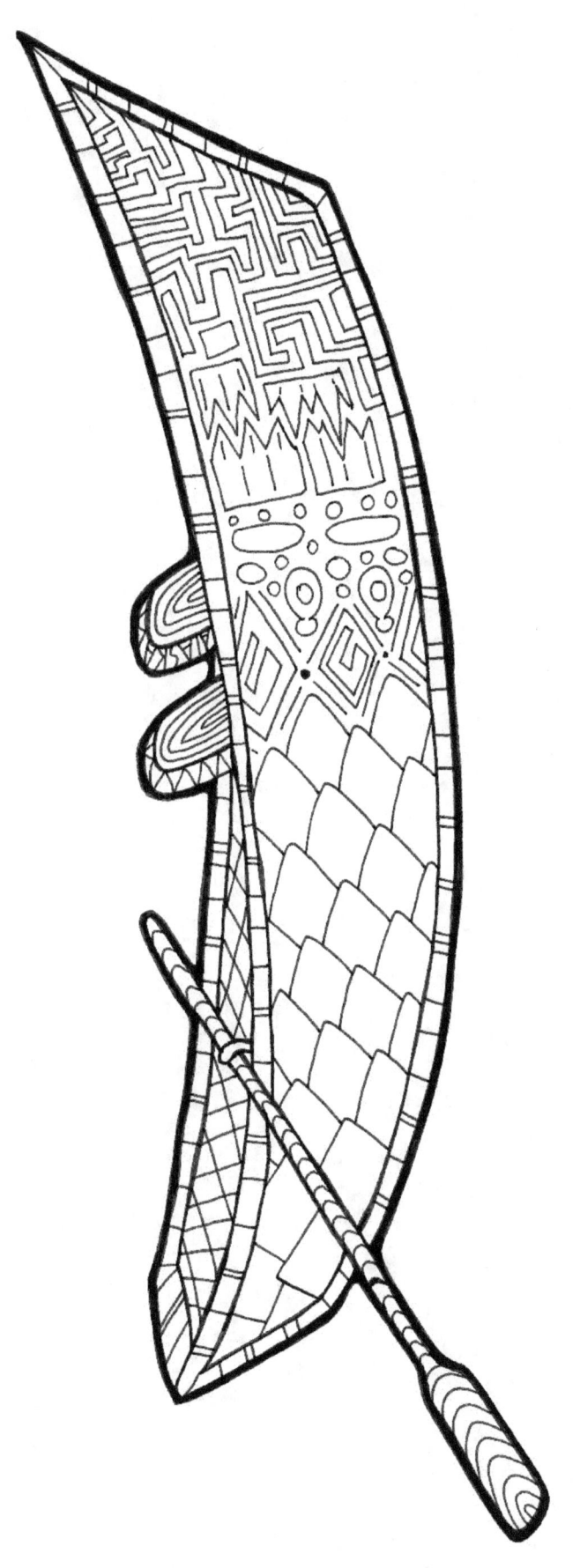

Drift Boat

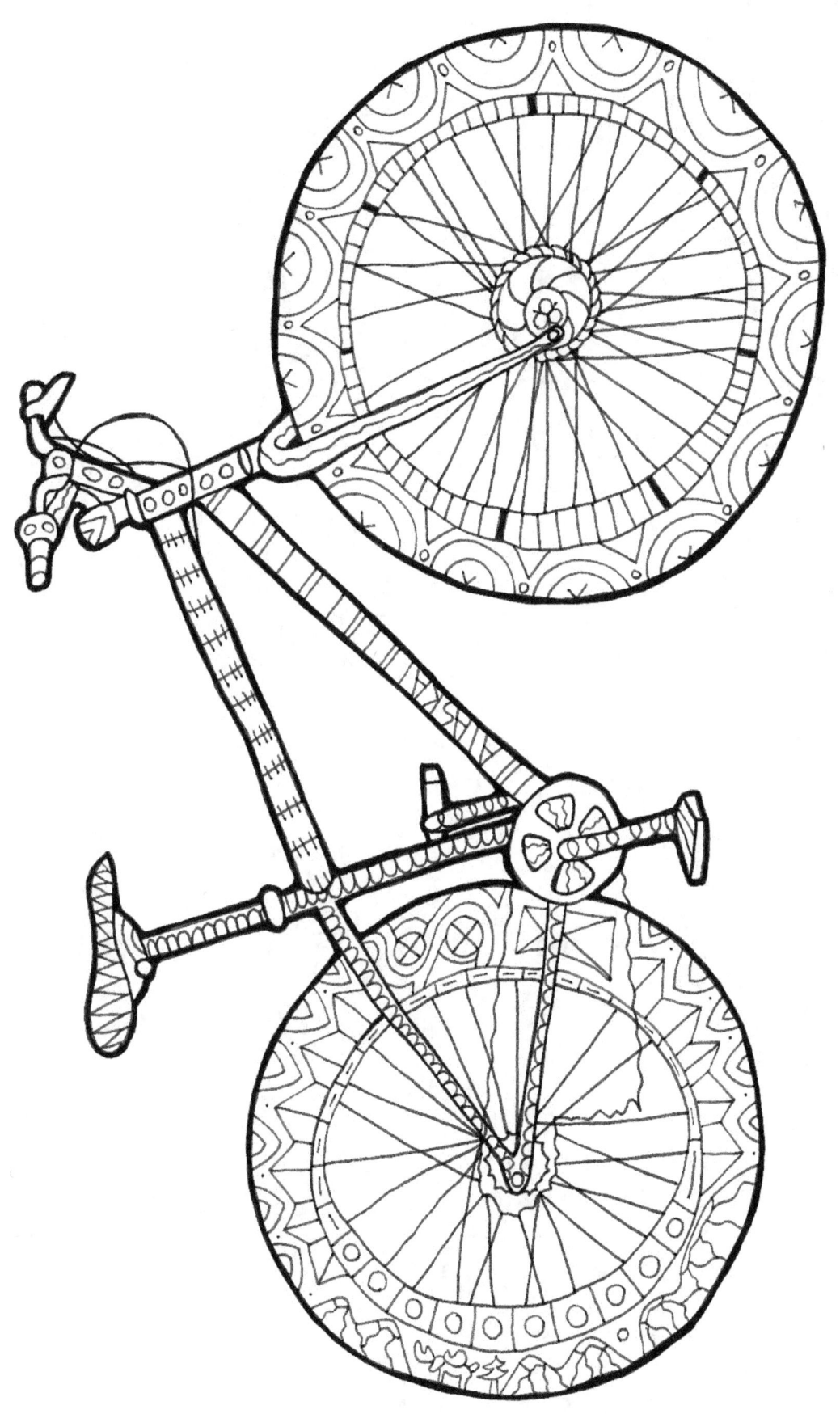

Fat Tire Bike

Great bike for riding in any weather, even snow

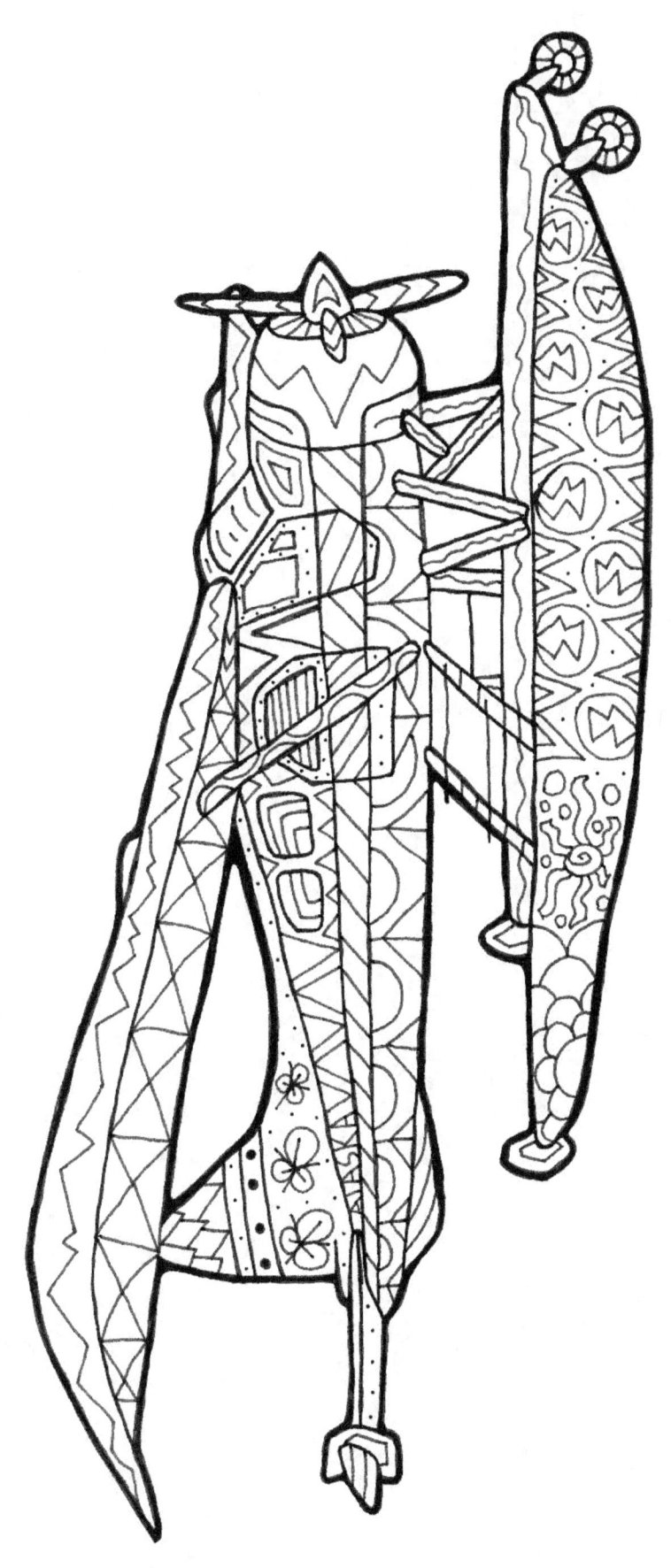

Float Plane

Some float planes can land on water OR land

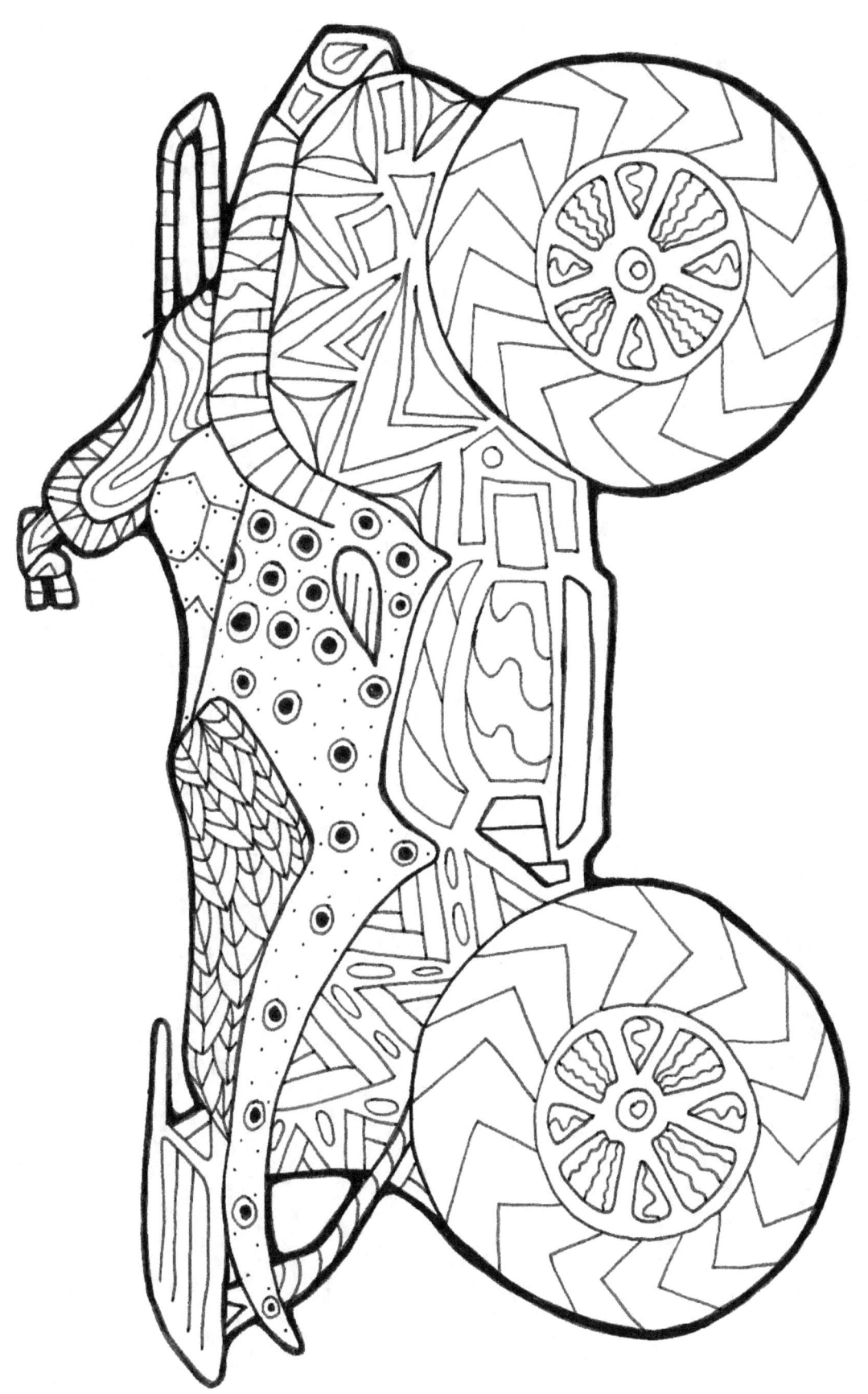

Four Wheeler or ATV

Many people use ATV's to get to areas not accessible by a standard motor vehicle. It is common to see them riding down the side of the road next to you.

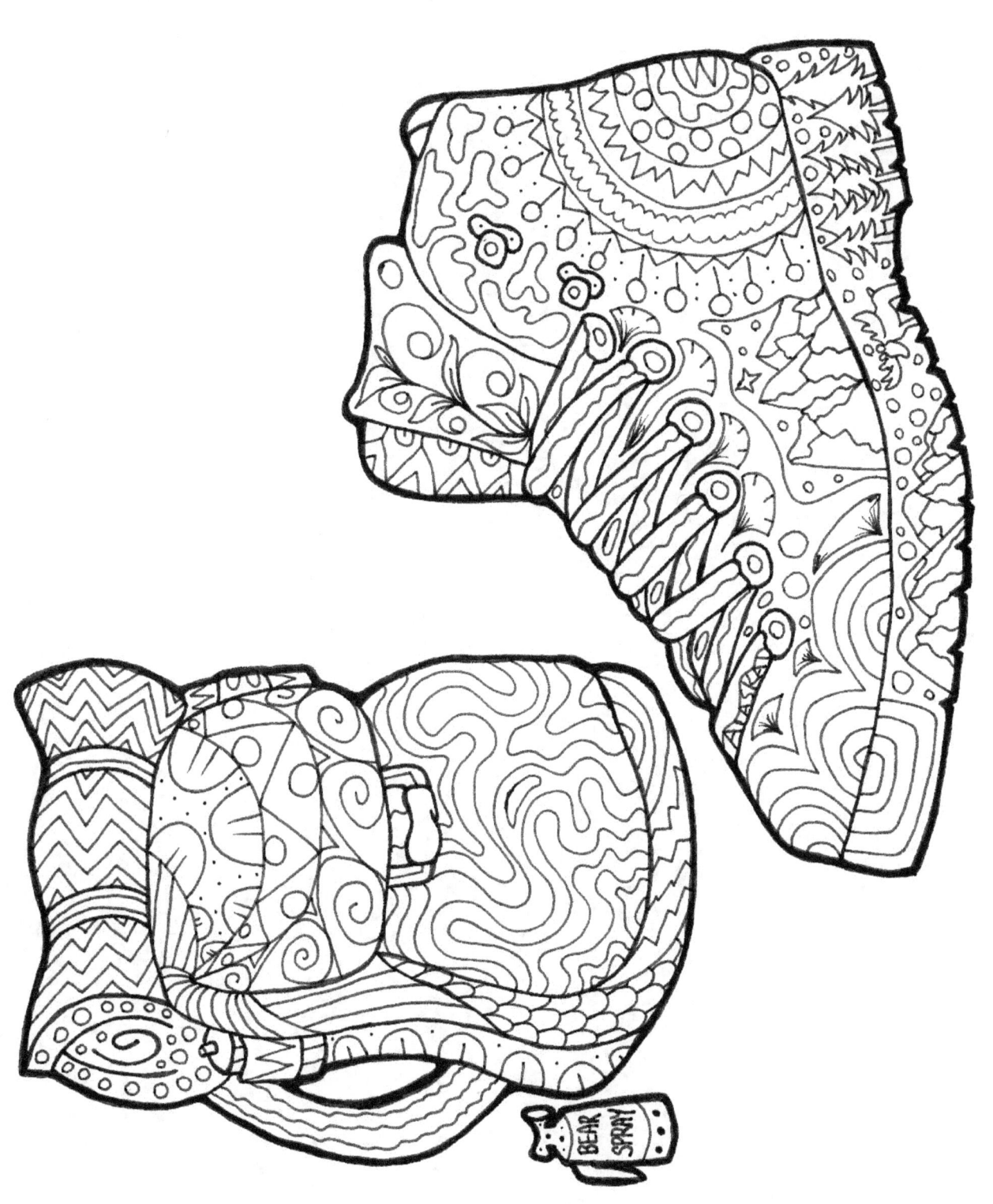

Hiking Boot and Backpack

There are over 750 hiking trails located around Alaska

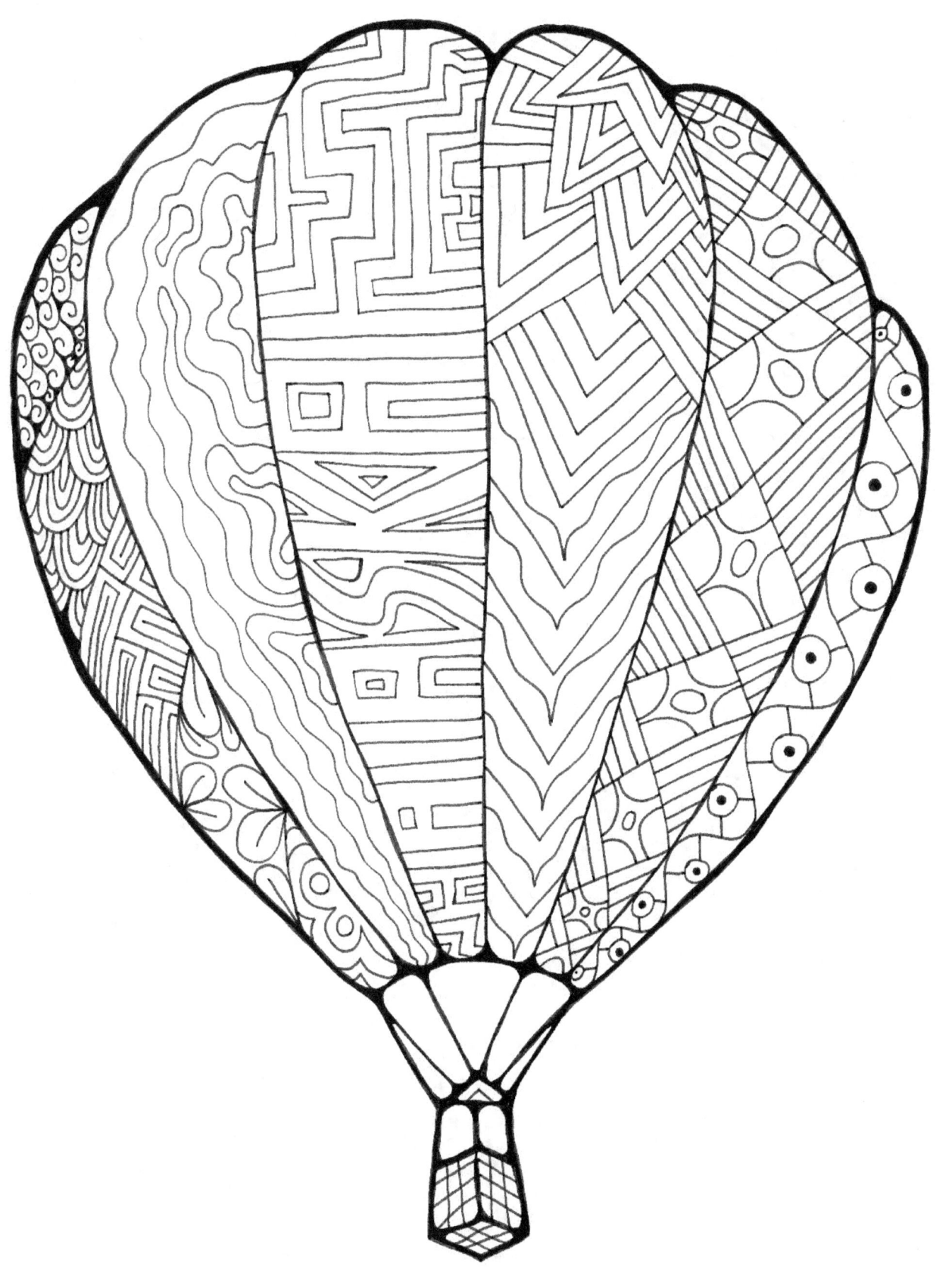

Hot Air Balloon

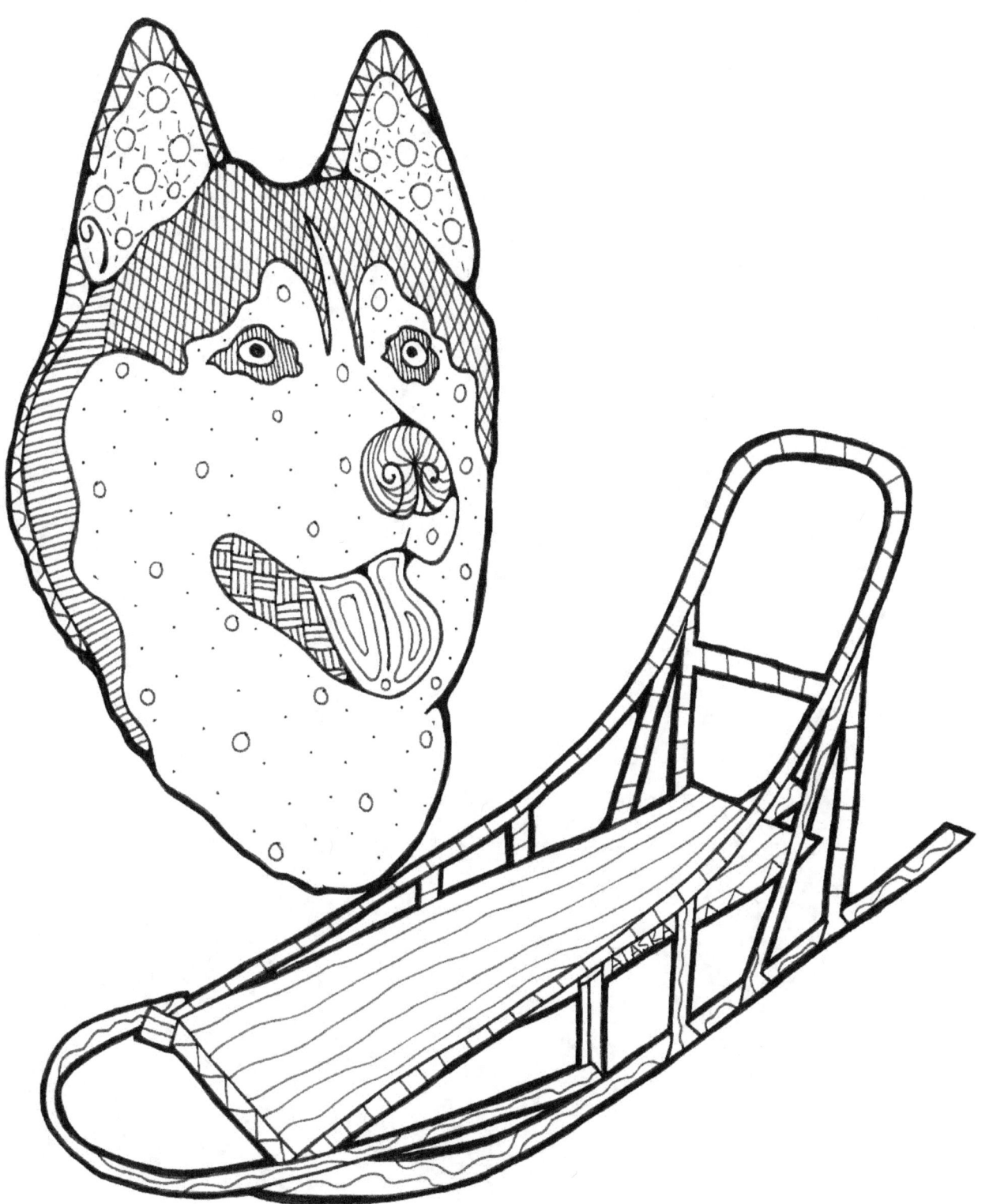

Husky with Sled

The Iditarod race starts in Anchorage and ends in Nome. The first race was run in March of 1973.

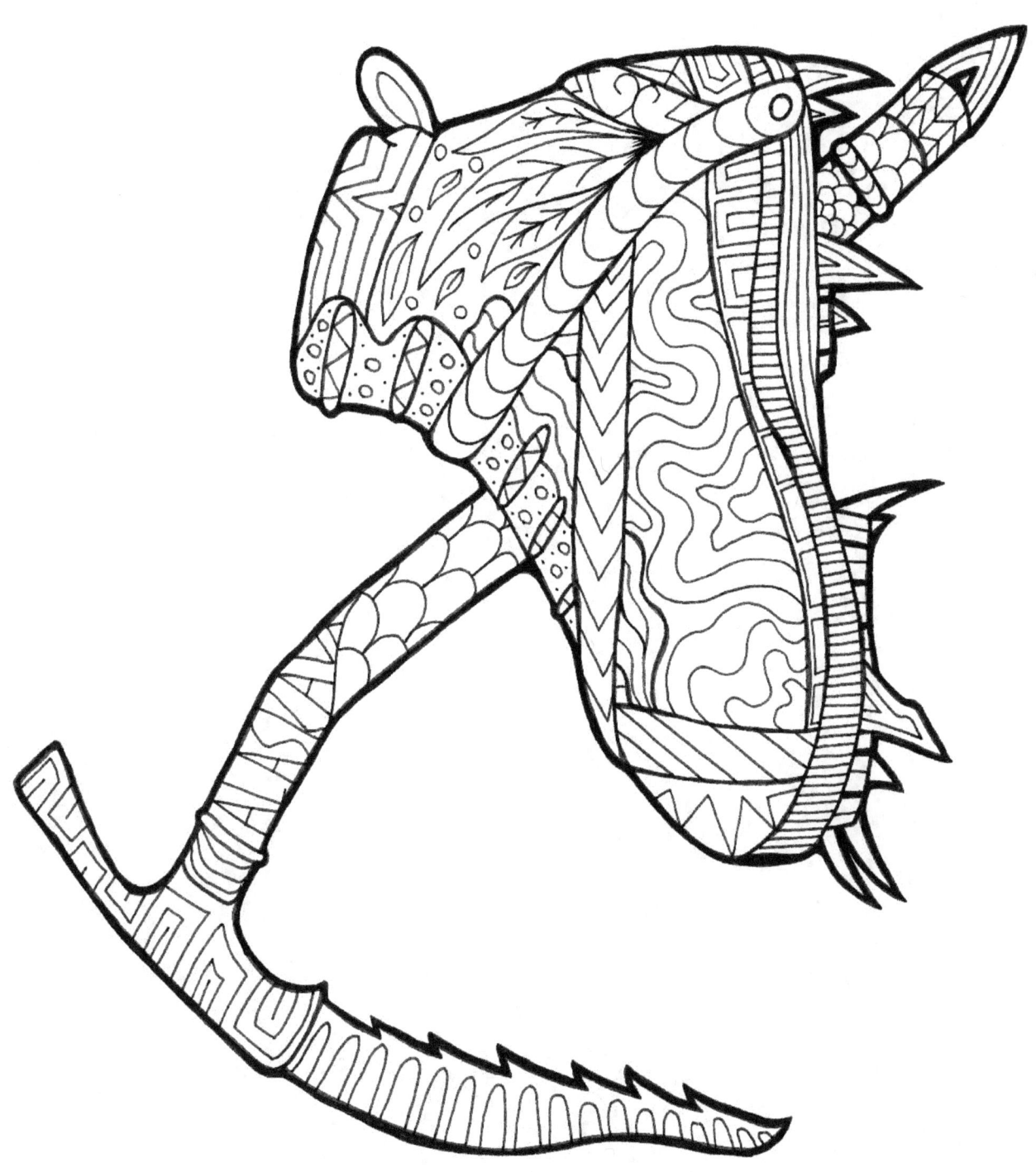

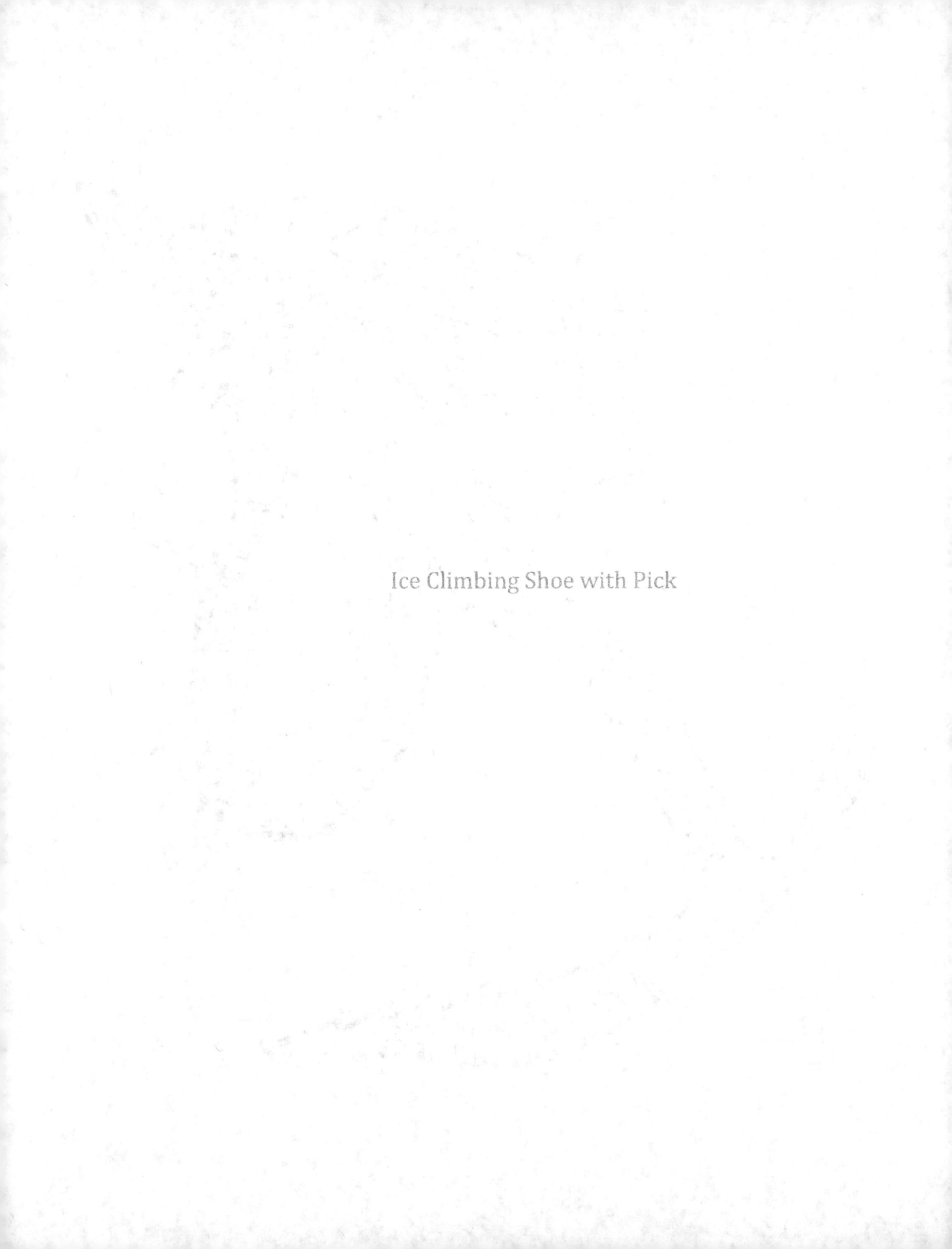

Ice Climbing Shoe with Pick

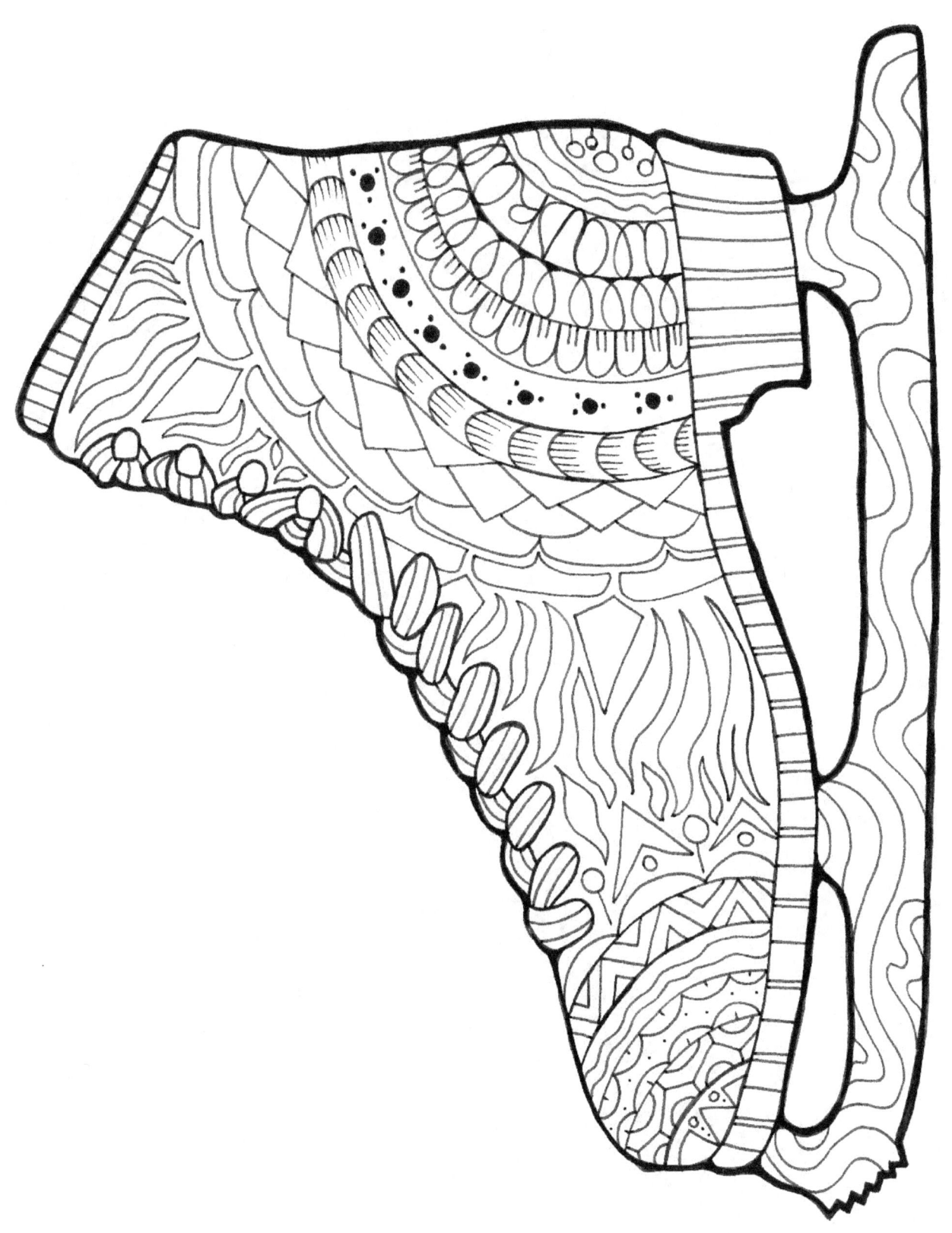

Ice Skate

In winter, many lakes freeze over and people ice skate on them.

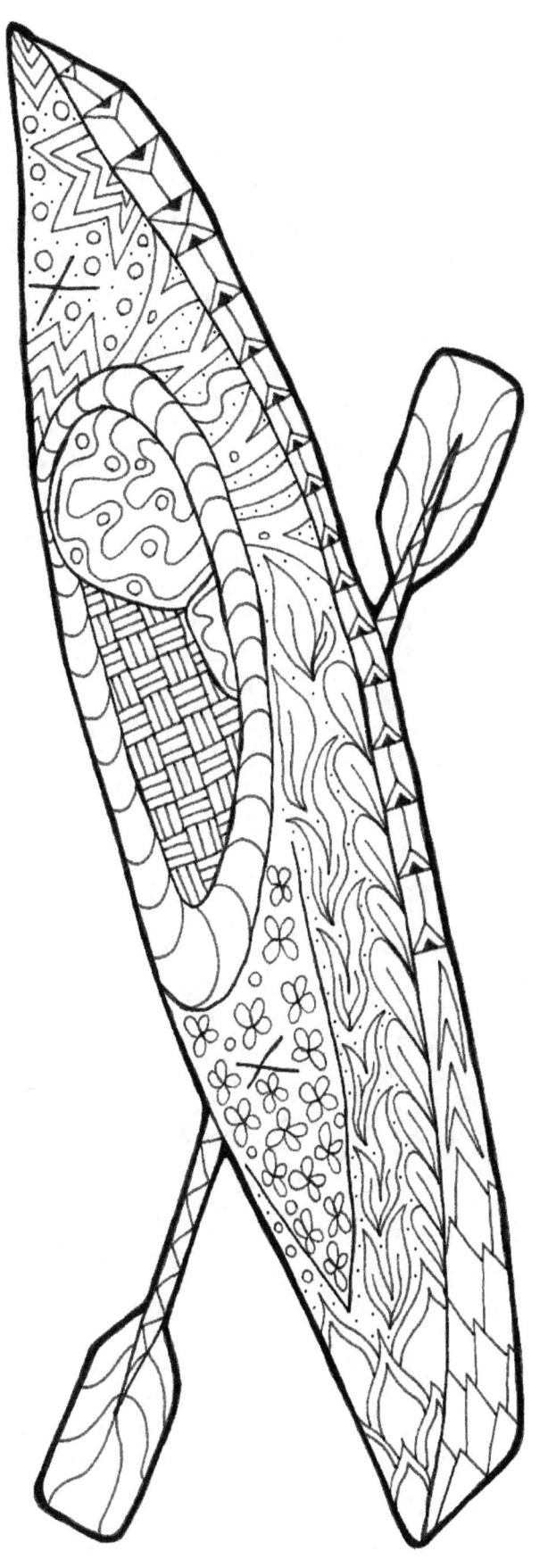

Kayak

There are many bodies of water to kayak on in Alaska with breathtaking views

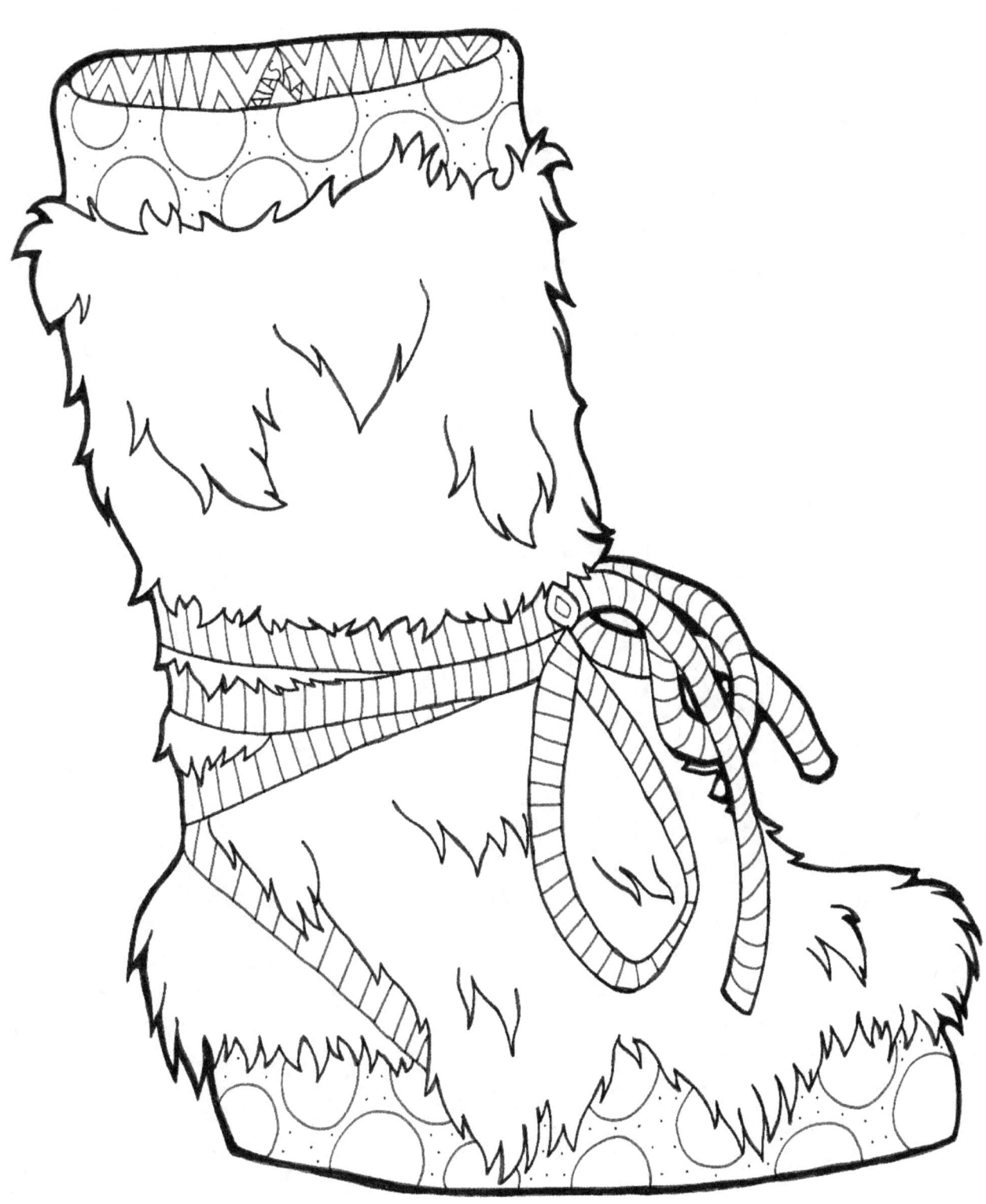

Mukluk

Mukluks are boots that were traditionally made from moose, caribou, or seal skin.

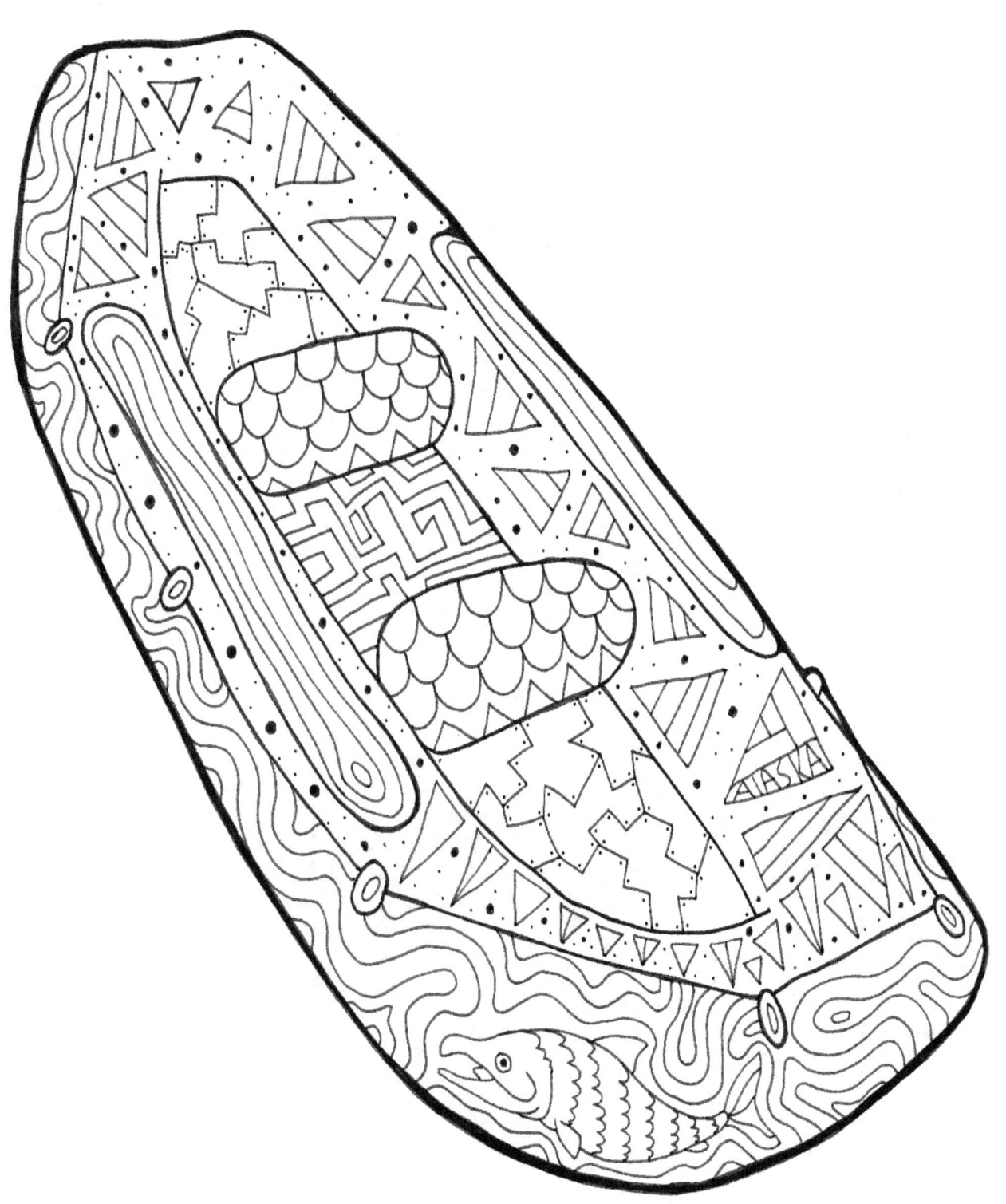

River Raft

There are many places that offer guided white water rafting in Alaska for the adventurous

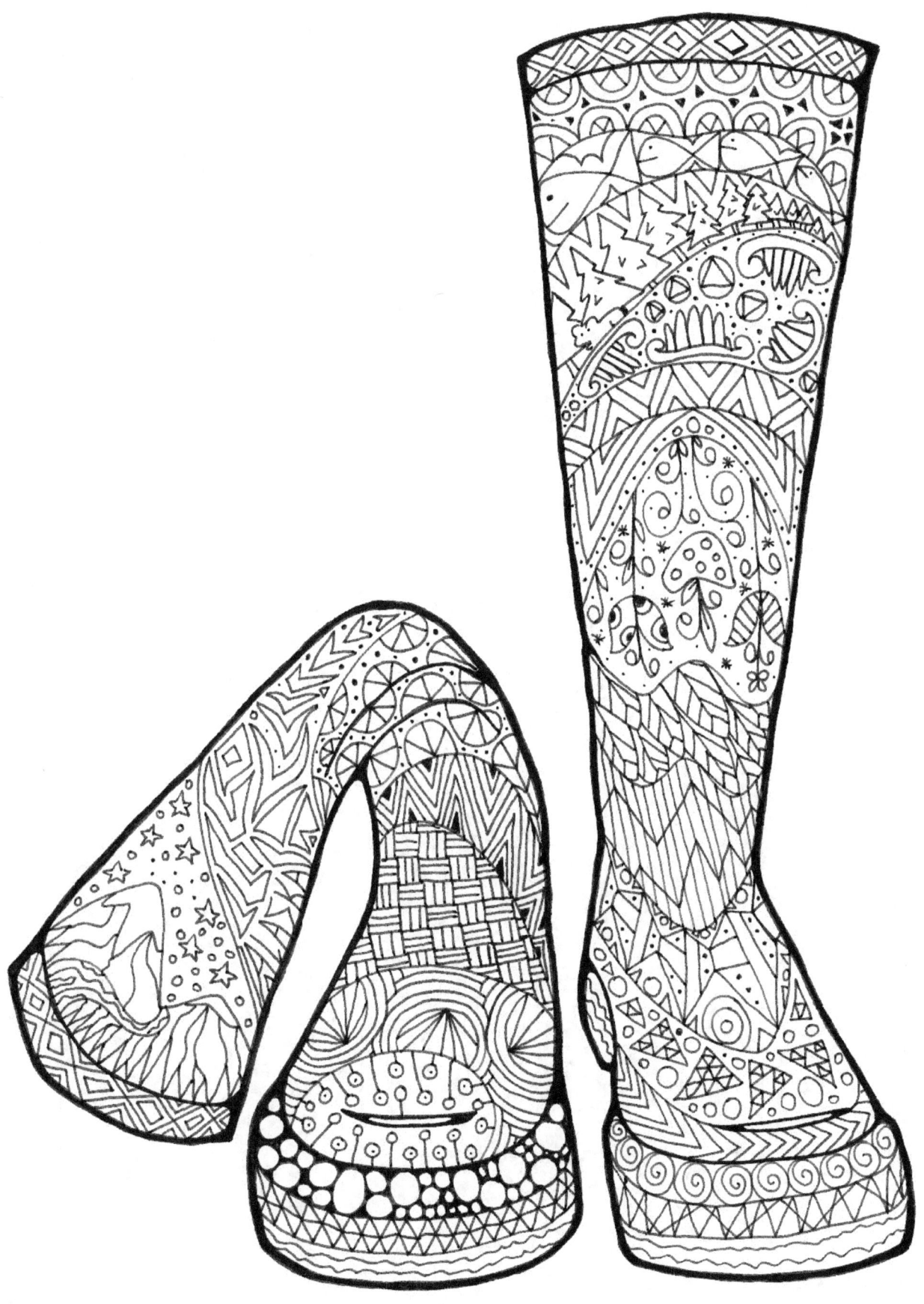

Rubber Boots

Rubber boots are a staple in many Alaskan's wardrobes.

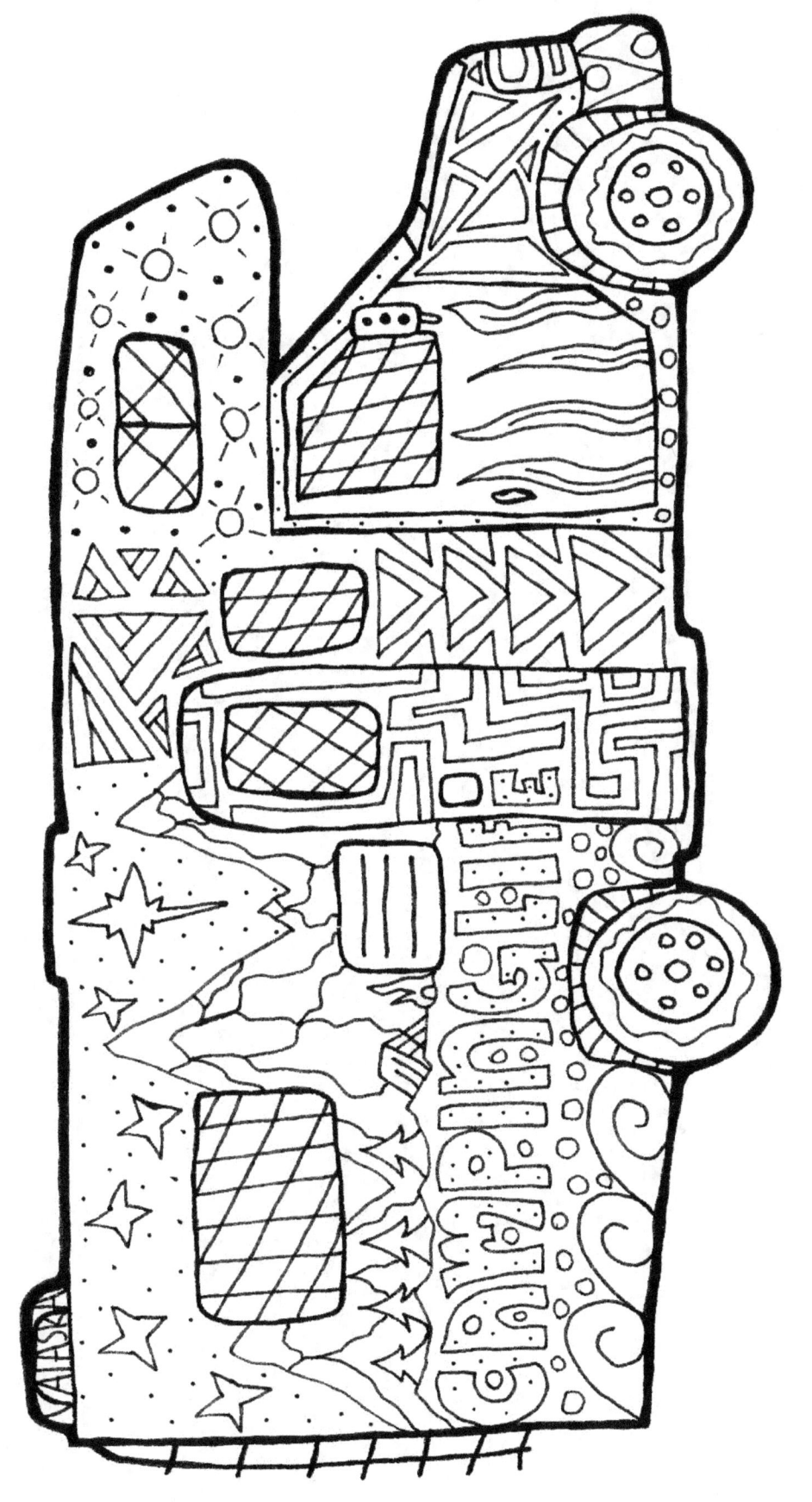

Recreational Vehicle

Many Alaskan's invest in RV's; there are a great many places to travel to and camp

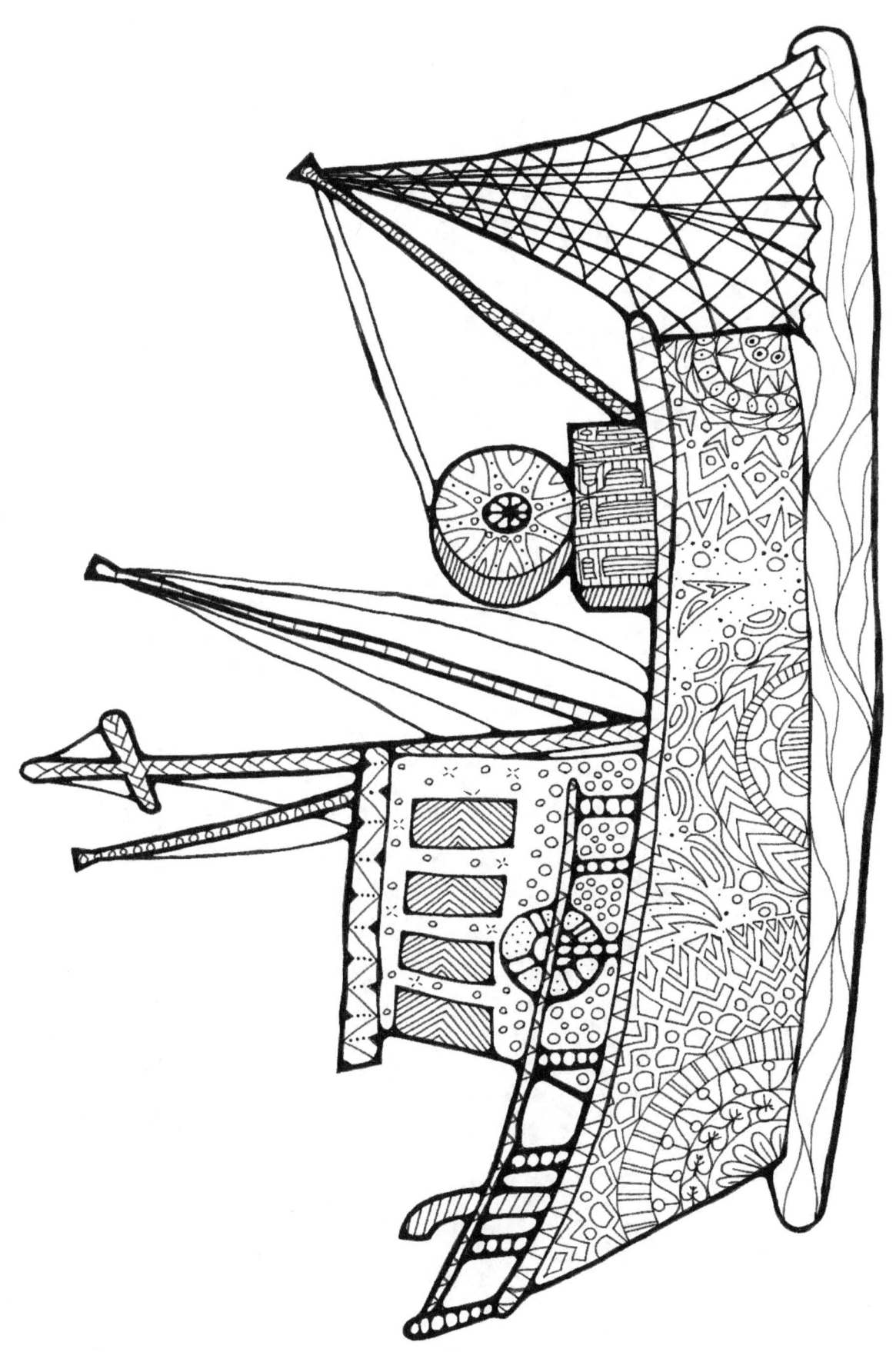

Seiner

A type of boat used in commercial fishing

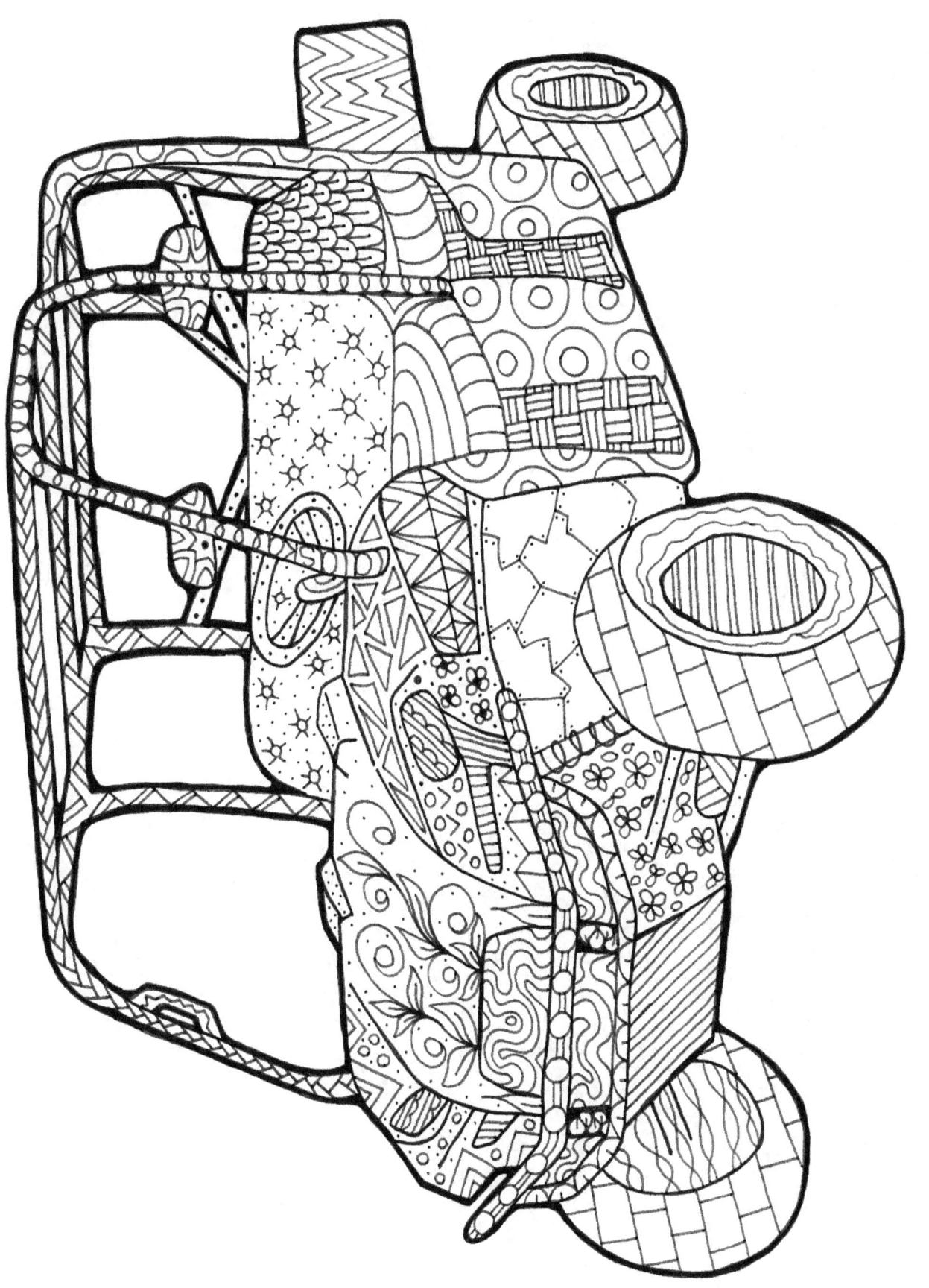

Side-by-side

Another off-road vehicle commonly seen alongside the roads and on trails

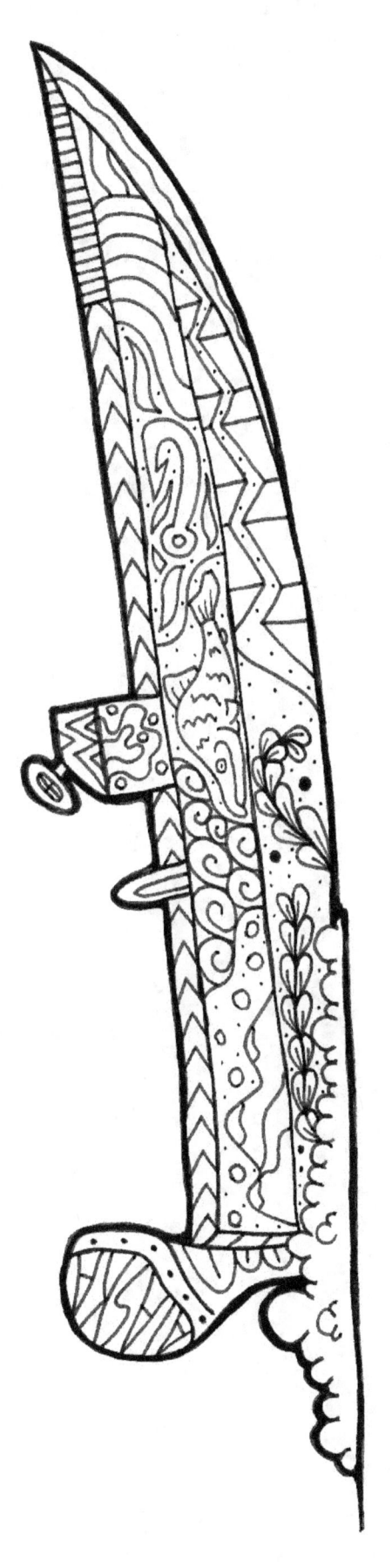

Skiff

Frequently used on Alaska's rivers to get to areas not accessible by vehicle

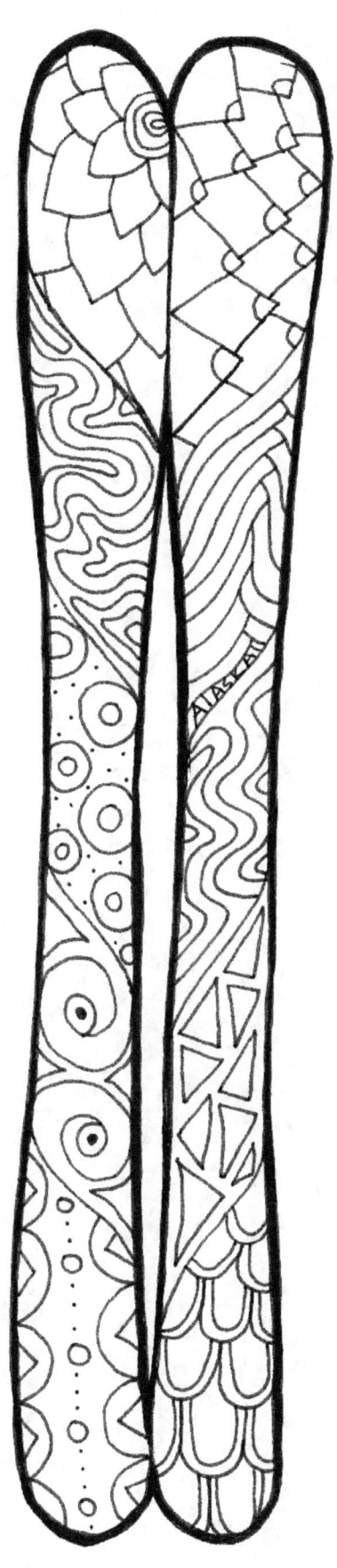

Skis

Skiing is an enjoyable pastime in the winter

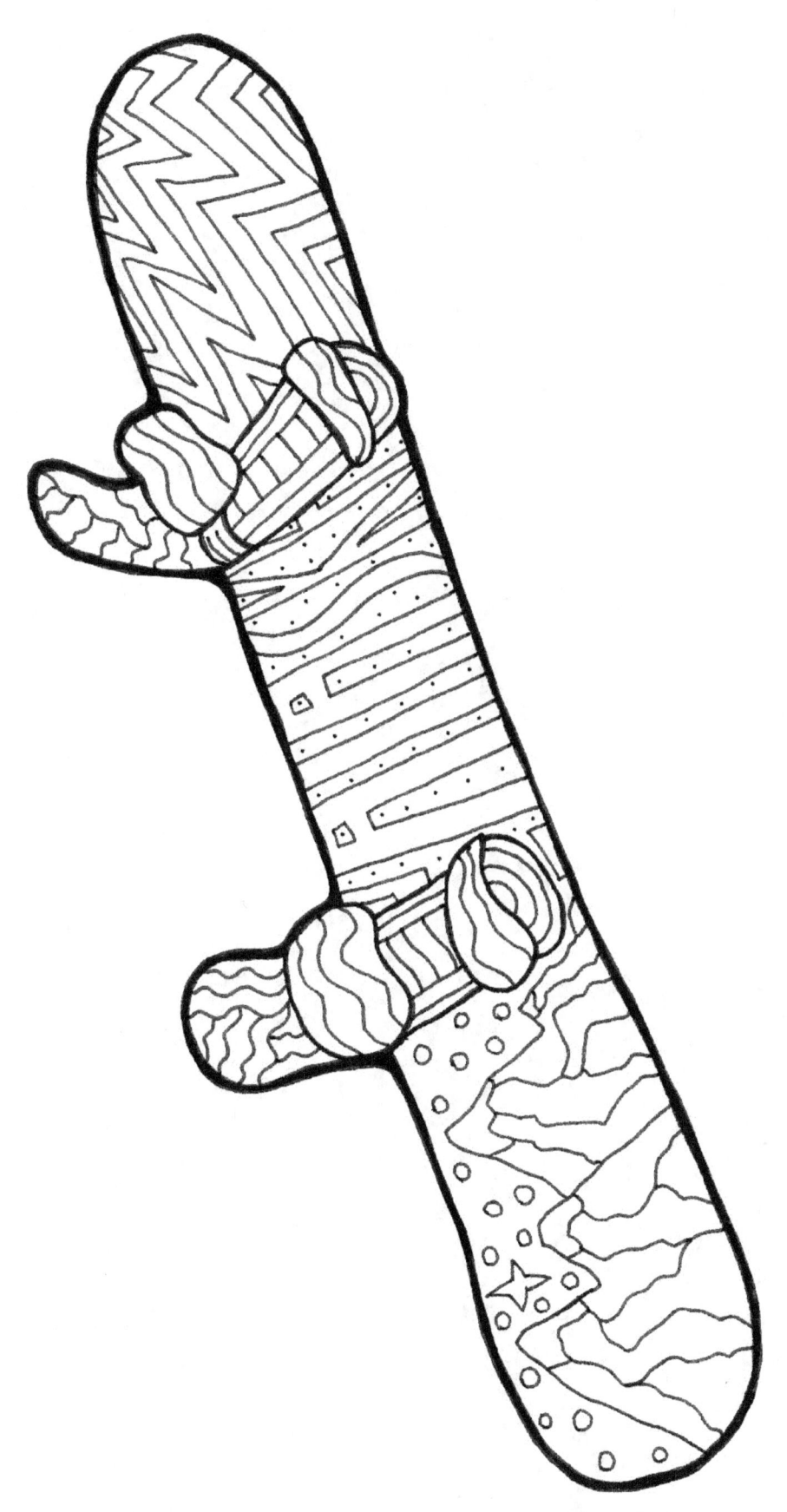

Snowboarding

Alaska offers many opportunities for snowboarding large mountains

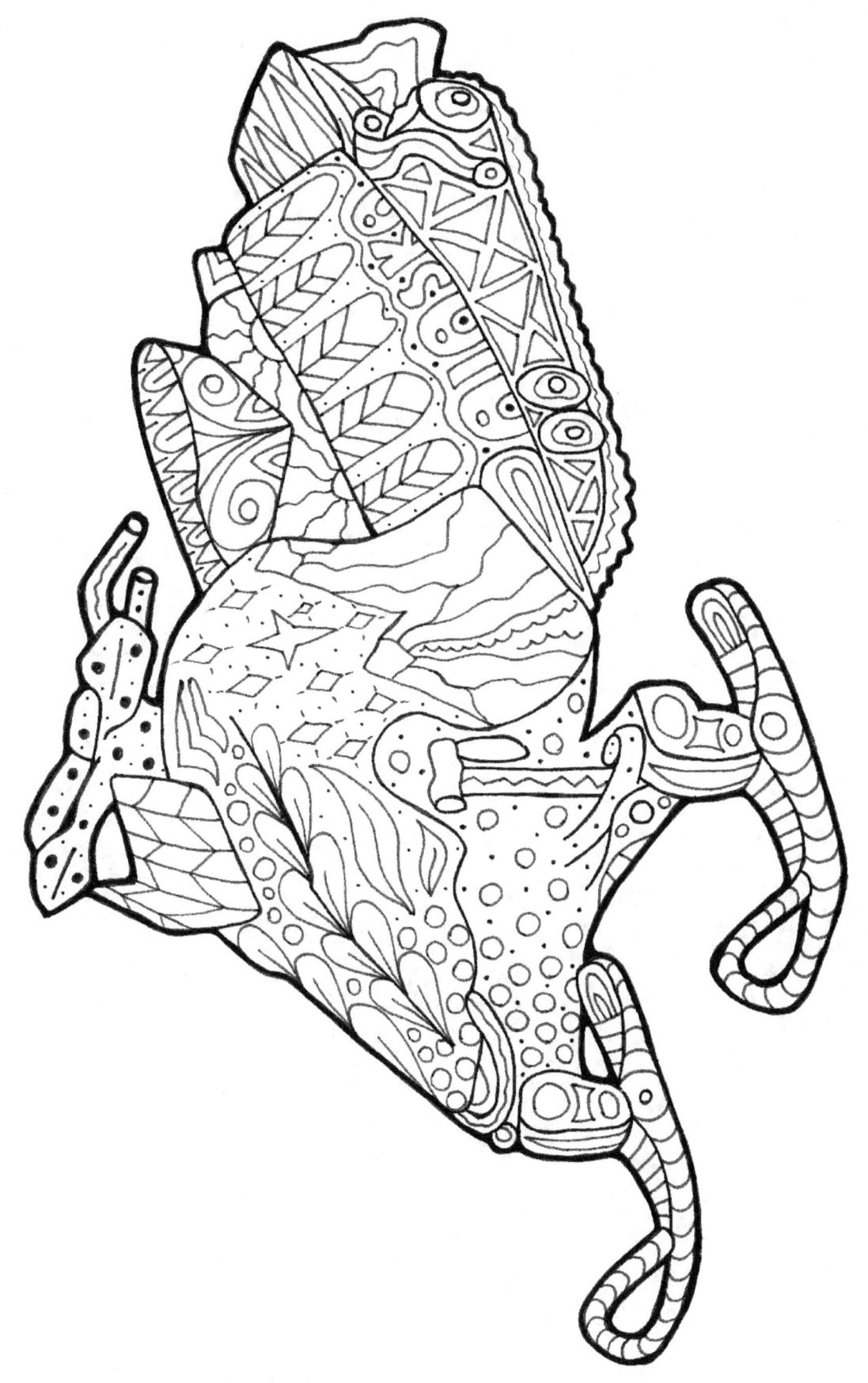

Snowmobile

Snowmobiles are known as 'snowmachines' or 'sleds' in Alaska

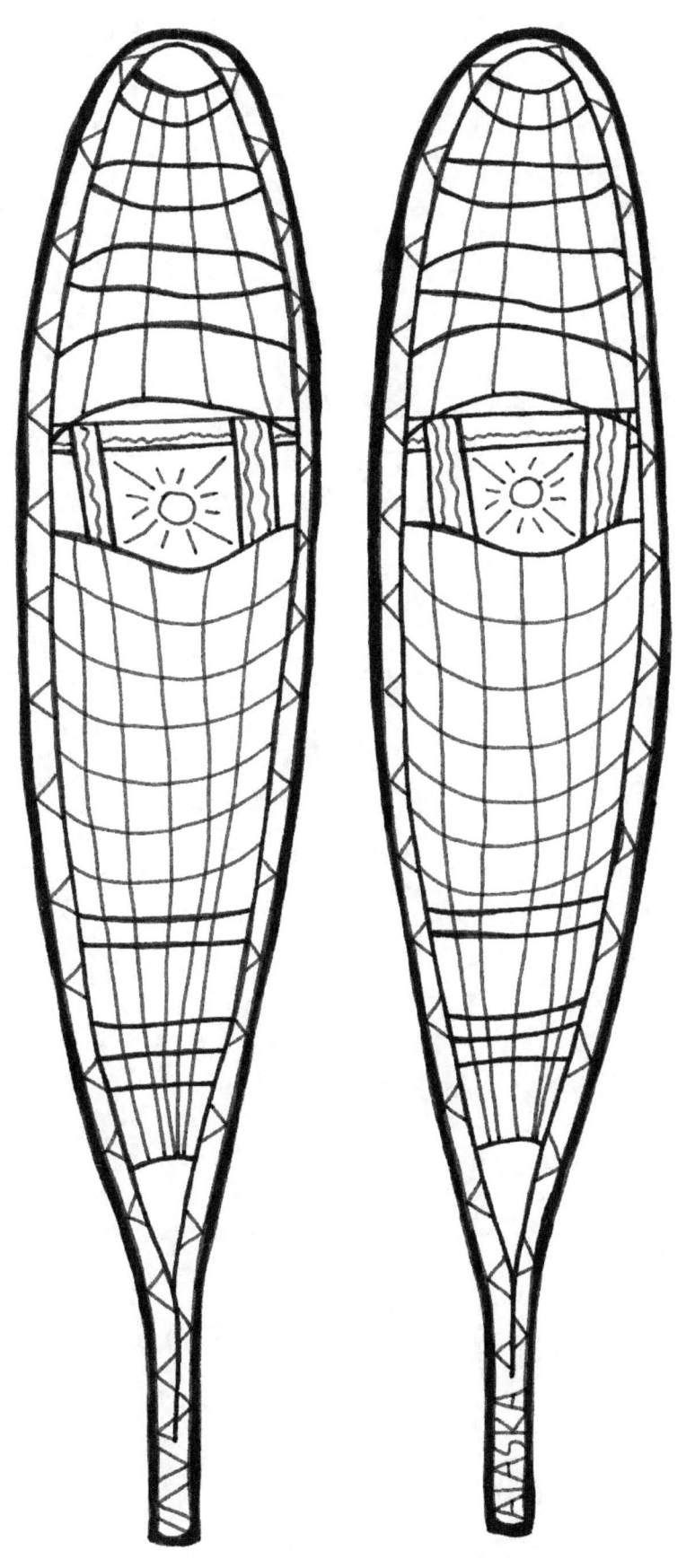

Alaskan Snowshoes

Snowshoes keep you from sinking into the snow due to the surface area the snowshoes cover

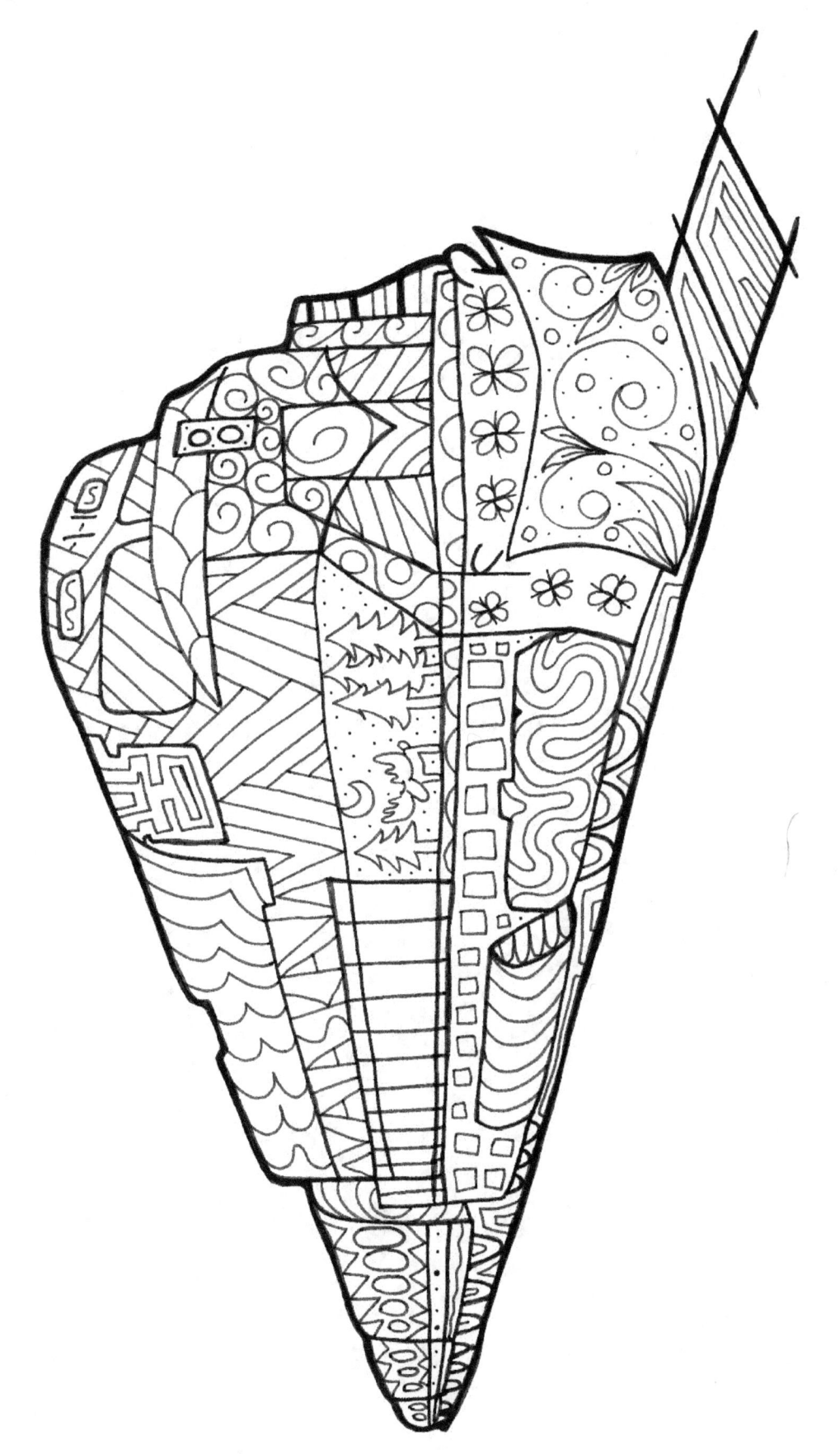

Train

The Alaska Railroad has a stretch of track from Seward to Fairbanks, about 470 miles

About the Artist

Brittney is a former Army brat, turned Alaskan artist currently residing in Wasilla, Alaska. She lives with her partner, their daughter, and their 3 cats: Socrates, Aristotle, and Sir Frances Bacon. Brittney has always been the creative one in her family, crafting since childhood. She began drawing her animals and other special projects over 5 years ago and finds it very soothing and rewarding. She hopes you find this coloring book as fun and relaxing as she does. To keep up with her future and present projects including stickers and prints, 'like' her page on Facebook:
www.facebook.com/artbybrittneyk

If you are interested in a custom drawing or prices on art prints, please e-mail inkedfoxak@gmail.com

Traveling Alaska: A Little Help

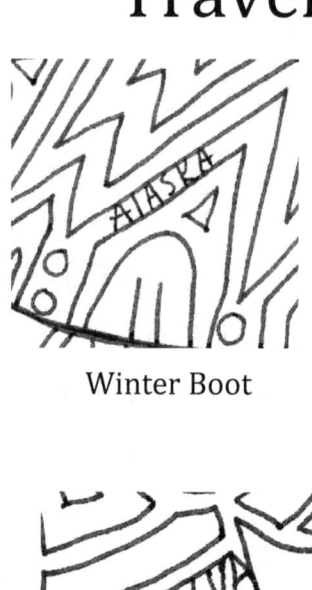
Winter Boot

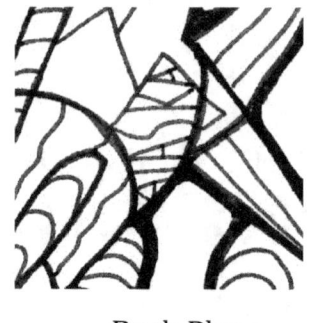
Bush Plane

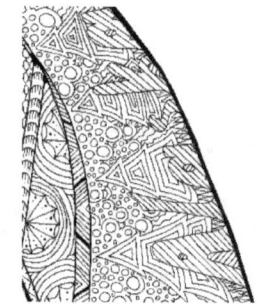
Canoe

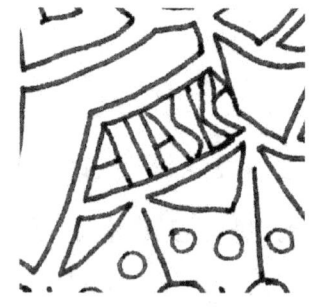
Climbing Shoe

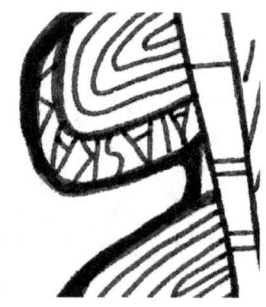
Drift Boat

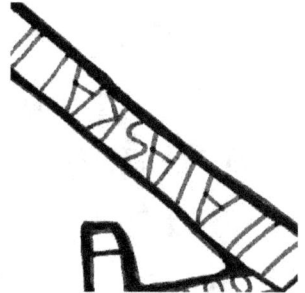
Fat Tire Bike

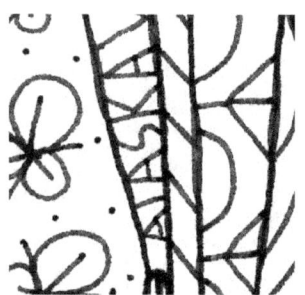
Float Plane

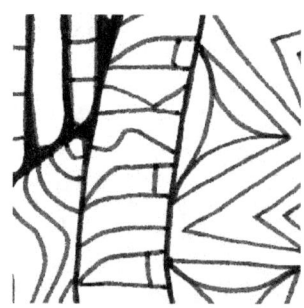
Four-Wheeler

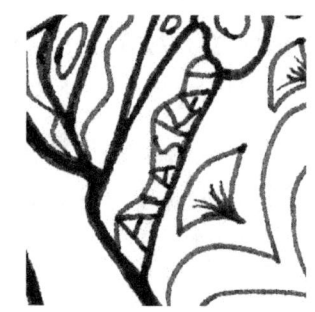
Hiking Boot with Backpack

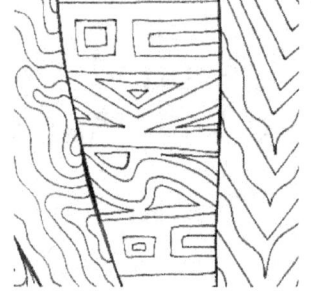
Hot Air Balloon

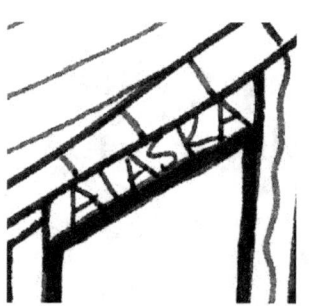
Huskie and Sled

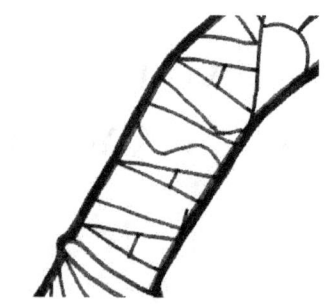
Ice Climbing Shoe and Pick

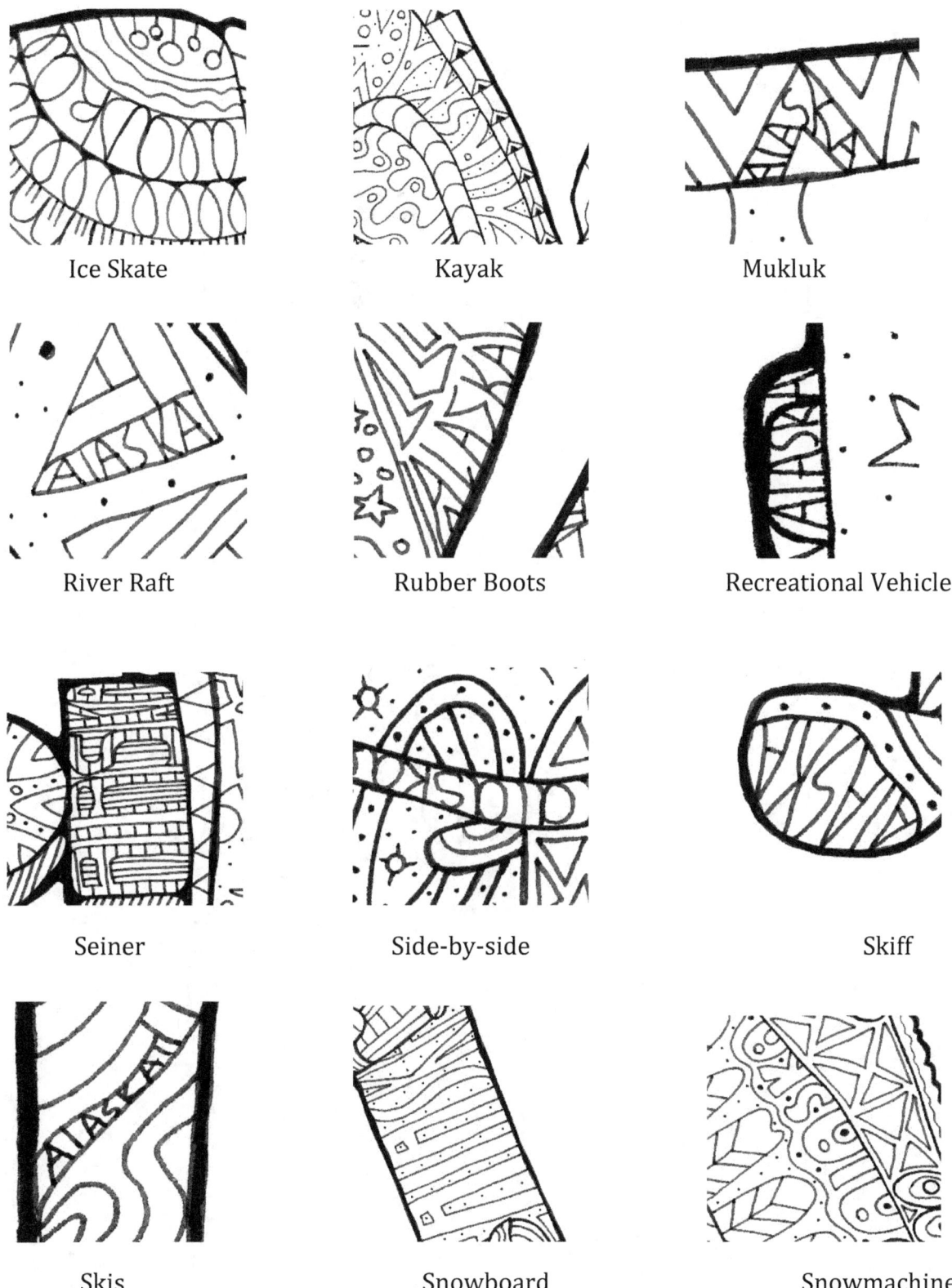

Ice Skate	Kayak	Mukluk
River Raft	Rubber Boots	Recreational Vehicle
Seiner	Side-by-side	Skiff
Skis	Snowboard	Snowmachine

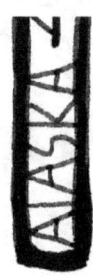

Alaskan Snowshoes

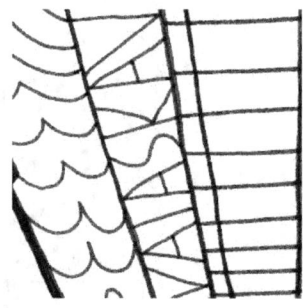

Train

www.ingramcontent.com/pod-product-compliance
Lightning Source LLC
Chambersburg PA
CBHW062340220526
45469CB00008B/2785